Testimonials

STUDENTS

"It was amazing to get the opportunity to work with Jean O'Toole. She was full of enthusiasm and that is one of the things that kept me motivated. When I thought about giving up, her drive to help us find scholarships is what made me stay. "
– Brittany C., 12th grade student

"Jean made students change their minds about giving up."
– Andres D., 12th grade student

"Jean helped me realize that anything is possible. Also, it has motivated me to do more."
– Johnathan Aviles, 12th grade student

"Mrs. O'Toole, thank you so much for helping me find scholarships with your *Scholarship Strategies.* It really has helped me with my money mission. I am now productive and motivated. I will continue my search for scholarships and can't wait to apply to the ones you helped me find. Thanks!"
– Kaitlyn L., 10th grade student

"There is no doubt that Jean O'Toole gives each and every one of us all her energy and support to keep us motivated. I thank her so much because if it weren't for her, I would only have a couple of scholarships on my personal spreadsheet."
– Katherine R., 12th grade student

T0151147

"Jean was helpful and provided a lot of resources which made searching for scholarships easier."
– **Kate M.**, 11th grade student

"Jean taught us things we never knew. "
– **Elizabeth B.**, 11th grade student

"You opened my mind to things I never knew. You truly taught me the lesson that if you are hungry for something, don't just starve – EAT. You truly inspire me. Thank you, Jean. I plan on being a success."
– **Sharday U.**, 12th grade student

"*Scholarship Strategies* has been helpful and encouraging. Never have I been so encouraged to apply for scholarships."
– **Rossely R.**, 12th grade student

"I loved her enthusiasm and how passionate she is about scholarships. She helped me look at scholarships in a different way."
– **Julissa M**, 12th grade student

"This was very helpful. You have inspired me to apply for many scholarships. You have encouraged me to do the best I possibly can to receive scholarships. Thank you for your encouragement."
– **Carmen P**, 12th grade student

"Jean, you really influenced me today because life is tough and it's not every day you get someone to give you advice for the future and life. Thank you."
– **Alaffia J.**, 12th grade student

EDUCATORS and SCHOOL COUNSELORS

"Jean, our 41 grads were all accepted into college and earned 5.6 million in scholarship funding. Thanks for your help! *Scholarship Strategies* is an asset."
– Anthony Degatano Ed.D,
Dean of Academics, Wildwood Catholic High School

"I was amazed with, not only the content, but Jean's inspirational approach. She knows exactly how to keep students engaged."
– Cynthia Russo,
Scholarship Consultant, High School of Art and Design

"*Scholarship Strategies* is informative, motivating and inspirational for students. Students responded extremely well to the process and approach."
– Michelle Noonan,
Assistant Principal, Peace and Diversity Academy

"*Scholarship Strategies* is fun and informative. It really provides helpful and valuable scholarship information and advice. Ms. O'Toole keeps the students involved and interested. The information is straight and to the point. It's simple so they remember the content. I already have students being proactive at my school."
– Keisha Morris,
Guidance Counselor, Bronx High School for the Visual Arts

"*Scholarship Strategies – Finding and Winning the Money You Need* is the most important tool a school can provide for students."
– Andrea Chappetta,
School Counselor, School for Community Research and Learning High School

"Students need to hear the messages that we try to bring to them and with powerful and energetic tools like *Scholarship Strategies*, they will hear it."
– Nancy Trapido,
College Access Counselor, Astor Collegiate Academy

"Jean lets students know exactly what they need. *Scholarship Strategies* provides the best format and we can find."
– Josh Javer,
Guidance Counselor, Pelham Preparatory Academy

BOOK STORES

"Jean has a great understanding of scholarships. Her message is informative, insightful and energized! Attendance at the book signing was larger than other 'name' authors."
– Donna Fell,
Owner, Sparta Books, Sparta NJ

Scholarship Strategies

Scholarship
STRATEGIES

Finding and Winning the Money You Need

Jean O'Toole

Scholarship Strategies
Finding and Winning the Money You Need
© 2020 Jean O'Toole

Published in New York, New York, by Morgan James Publishing. Morgan James is a trademark of Morgan James, LLC. www.MorganJamesPublishing.com

ISBN 9781642794823 paperback

ISBN 9781642794830 eBook

Library of Congress Control Number: 2019933449

Design by:
Design by Misty Wilt Graphic Design LLC
www.mistywilt.com

Illustrations by:
Illustrations by Michael A. Zug
realzugart@gmail.com

Morgan James is a proud partner of Habitat for Humanity Peninsula and Greater Williamsburg. Partners in building since 2006.

Get involved today! Visit
MorganJamesPublishing.com/giving-back

To the thousands of high school, college,
and career counselors who work so hard to
guide young people toward their dreams.
I applaud your commitment to helping students
and parents, despite your work load that seems
to grow with each academic year. Your drive
to help your students find their way is truly
admirable work and I honor you for it. On behalf
of the entire team at Connections101, thank you
for NOT GIVING UP ON ANY STUDENT.

FOREWORD

As a long-time educator and Director of Internships at Cathedral High School, I have partnered with administration to help prepare hundreds of our young women for their next phase in life. After all their hard work in achieving good grades, participating in activities, and giving back to the community, one of the BIGGEST CHALLENGES they will face is paying for their next phase of education.

Students know how college can affect their world, open doors to new experiences, and lead them to successful careers. It is scary not knowing how you will afford the high cost and wondering if the road is paved with heavy debt.

This is where Jean O'Toole has been a tremendous asset. For the past ten years, Jean has spoken to our seniors. Her knowledge of scholarships is vast and her ability to simplify the process of seeking financial aid is most impressive. Furthermore, her energy and enthusiasm have been contagious.

When she presents at our assemblies, students are consistently engaged. You can see their eyes open wide, as they feel a sense of HOPE FOR THEIR COLLEGE FUTURE.

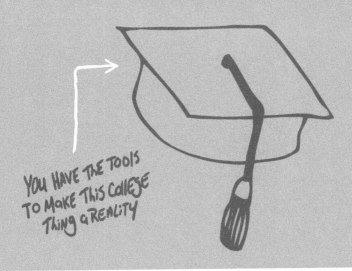

YOU HAVE THE TOOLS TO MAKE THIS COLLEGE Thing a REALITY

I was thrilled to learn that Jean decided to put her wealth of knowledge into print. *Scholarship Strategies* is an invaluable resource that shares insights beyond what most can provide. Assistance is out there. You just need to know where to look. Scholarships are offered by hundreds of colleges, corporations, agencies, and individuals.

Scholarship Strategies educates on how to sift through a sea of scholarship opportunities; how to leverage one's own skills, experience, and assets to qualify for scholarships; and how to apply and appeal for aid. It offers step-by-step guidance that answers many questions and relieves much of the stress.

Guidance and admissions counselors are powerful allies. However, the onus is on students and their families to make college a reality. This book leaves readers, our next generation, empowered to take action and EXCITED FOR THE POSSIBILITIES that lie ahead.

Marguerite Kiely
Chairperson of the Business and Careers Department
Cathedral High School, New York City

CONTENTS

MY MONEY MISSION COMMITMENT

Choice. It is the most powerful thing I own. My decisions will either open doors or close them. Beginning this second, I choose to start my scholarship Money Mission. My mission begins right now. Minute one. My commitment:

I AM WORTH THE EFFORT. My goals and my dreams are worth the effort. I refuse to resign myself to years, decades, or a lifetime of paying off college debt. I have it within my own ability to find scholarship money for college. I am willing to commit my time and energy. I have the will to try. I know that ultimately it is up to me alone to follow through. I recognize that action and inaction are both powerful forces. Today, I am taking action—I am choosing to begin, because I AM WORTH IT.

My Money Mission begins today _____
DATE

Signed _____

1

REPEAT!

#'s game

INCREASE Odd!

Big 6

CHOOSE!

Chapter One

GET READY TO START YOUR MONEY MISSION

Congratulations on your courage! You are embarking on a quest to find the money you need for college. You have catapulted ahead of most students by taking on this mission. You are a revolutionary!

Like most students, you know you need money for college. The traditional route—applying for financial aid with the FAFSA, searching the internet for additional scholarships, and playing the Waiting Game (more on that in a minute)— might seem like a good plan, but this process is no longer ideal. College loan debt is on the rise, and this system is inadequate for the rapidly rising costs of higher education.

You want a different result. You need a different plan. Our approach to scholarship searching will open doors to unbelievable outcomes.

STEP OUTside the Box

Get ready, because you are about to step up your game—big time. You are going to rise above the crowd with this new approach. You and *you alone* will determine the limits of what you can achieve.

Ultimately, you will hold on to this mantra: **If it is to be, it is up to me.**

A Commitment to Possibility

The Money Mission requires you to commit to:

- 🪙 *Get organized*
- 🪙 *Stay focused*
- 🪙 *Research a myriad of resources (beyond the obvious ones)*

To accomplish your mission, you will have to work hard. You know that "if it is to be, it is up to me."

On the other hand, students without a Money Mission choose to wait. They wait to be told, wait to be given, wait to be shown scholarship opportunities by a school counselor or parent. They are playing what we call the Waiting Game.

Only you can decide whether to play the Waiting Game or commit to a Money Mission. Your future is at stake!

Consider the following: Your parents most likely possess the same knowledge and experience as you in this process. They might also be going through this process for the first time. And while your school counselors are there to assist you, they are also busy assisting *every other student*. They are busy professionals with many priorities other than you.

From here on out, any time someone—your counselor, parent, anyone—gives you a scholarship application, consider it a bonus. After all, this is your dream, your future, your life. You control all of it.

Your Scholarships, Your Life

The key to staying out of the Waiting Game is to envision the end goal for your Money Mission. As an exercise, consider *your* answer to the statement:

I want scholarship money because . . .

Your reasons might include:

...my parents don't have a lot of money.

...I want the prestige that comes from winning certain scholarships.

...I don't want to have student loan debt.

...I don't have a college fund.

...I want to distinguish myself from other applicants when applying to elite programs.

All of these statements are valid and very important. Higher education is more expensive than ever. Unemployment and other financial burdens make the cost of college a struggle for many families. In the United States, student loan debt is at crisis proportions. But there is more to consider. Your Money Mission is much bigger than filling financial gaps or earning status. You need scholarship money because YOU NEED CHOICES. These choices can open up a world of possibilities to you. For example:

Outside scholarships come from individuals, organizations, companies, and foundations. These scholarships are not associated with a college or university or the government.

- *Scholarship money gives you the ability to go to your first choice school (if your grades and credentials will gain admission).*

- *Scholarship money means choosing where—the city or town, the country or state—you want to study.*

- *Scholarship money means you choose how to allocate any money you or your parents have saved, whether it's to pay for graduate school, the down payment on your first house, or seed money to launch your dream business. The possibilities are endless.*

- *Scholarship money gives you freedom from working long hours while in school, giving you more time for the things that matter—studying, extracurricular activities, volunteer and internship opportunities, and time with friends.*

The bottom line is that **scholarship money allows you to make choices based on the pursuit of personal fulfillment** rather than mere survival.

I have always had to fend for myself. I couldn't count on my parents because of addiction and incarceration. Somehow I've managed to pass my classes and keep my head up. I want to apply for scholarships and go to college. Truthfully though, I've always felt like *I am waiting around* for a handout when it comes to scholarships. Now I know I've got to make it *my business* to make my dreams come true. My Money Mission is to apply to every type of scholarship I can find.

—Selena C., 12th Grade Student

Did You Know?

Student loan debt in the U.S. is on the rise. In 2015, almost 71 percent of bachelor's degree recipients graduated with student loans. Ten years earlier, that number was 64 percent. And 20 years earlier, less than half of all students left college with loans.

YEAR	%	AVERAGE DEBT AT GRADUATION
2015	71%	$37,672
2005	64%	$20,976
1995	<50%	$12,255

Source: Mark Kantrowitz, Edvisors

As you work on your Money Mission, you must continually revisit *your* ideas about *your* future. Your priorities might evolve over time—and that's normal—but right now, close your eyes and imagine yourself walking across the campus of your dreams. Picture how you want your life to play out. Does your vision include the opportunities that open to you through scholarships?

Use your Money Mission to expand your possibilities. *Embrace this mission as your own personal responsibility.* You will likely have some help along the way—from this book, from your parents, from

Stack the Money

Stack as many outside scholarships as possible.

your friends, from your school—but your future is in your hands alone. In the end, it is ultimately up to you to create the life you really want.

This book will give you tools and strategies to help you find and systematically apply for outside scholarships. By working on your Money Mission, you can avoid the pitfalls of the old Waiting Game and head into the college and life of your dreams! YOU OWN YOUR OUTCOME!

you've got this!

8

Consider the choices you would make if scholarship money became available to you.

What would your college experience look like?

How would scholarships impact your life after college?

How would scholarships affect your family?

In Chapter 1, you turned a new leaf in life. You're off to a great start!

- ☑ You have committed to your Money Mission.

- ☑ You are not playing the Waiting Game.

- ☑ You know that your choices will determine your options.

Chapter Two

THE TRUTH ABOUT OUTSIDE SCHOLARSHIPS

When it comes to outside scholarships, there's a bevy of misinformation out there that can hinder your process. Every day, there are students who do not take action toward their Money Mission because they have heard or have been given false information about the availability of scholarship funds.

MYTHS

+

INACTION

=

MISSED

OPPORTUNITIES

Thankfully, there are many more scholarship opportunities than you might guess. Do not allow myths to get in the way of your mission! The only way to successfully implement your Money Mission is to bust some common scholarship myths and empower yourself with the facts.

MYTHS

SCHOLARSHIP MYTH 1: You can only get scholarships for **academic merit and athletics**.

FACT: Although many outside scholarships are awarded for academic merit and athletics, you will find many other scholarships awarded for a variety of other accomplishments. As you begin your Money Mission, you will find a vast quantity of scholarship offerings. You will discover that a host of organizations award scholarships to honor community service projects or exceptional leadership. Other scholarships may recognize special skills, characteristics, or interests. You may even find scholarships that are given to high school students just for being on track to graduate!

MONEY FOR MY UNIQUE TRAITS

SCHOLARSHIP MYTH 2: I have been offered a full-ride scholarship so **I don't need more money**.

FACT: Congratulations on that full ride! Even if it is to the university of your dreams, you may need more money for incidentals. Additional scholarship money could help you pay for meals not covered by room and board, buy a laptop computer, travel to see your family during breaks, or fulfill your dream of a semester abroad. Your Money Mission does not necessarily end with a full-ride scholarship.

SCHOLARSHIP MYTH 3: I don't qualify for scholarships because **my parents make too much money.**

FACT: Even if your family lives in a gold-plated palace and you don't actually need a dime, you can still win money for college. With the exception of need-based scholarships, income does not typically affect outside scholarship eligibility.

SCHOLARSHIP MYTH 4: To apply for scholarships, you **must be a high school senior.**

FACT You can find scholarships at every stage in life. Although the majority of college-bound students start the scholarship process toward the end of high school, outside scholarships are available to students of all ages—whether you are in kindergarten or over 30.

Good To Know!

Scholarships awarded to younger students are usually disbursed in one of two ways:

- as a check issued directly to the family, or

- as a bond that matures when the student turns 18.

SCHOLARSHIP MYTH 5: My window to apply for scholarships **ends when I graduate** from high school.

FACT Your window doesn't magically end the moment you receive your high school diploma. Believe it or not, you can apply for outside scholarships *while* you are in college. You may be able to use funds toward tuition, loan payments, or other expenses. Remember: there are scholarship opportunities for every stage in life and every level of higher education, whether you are attending a technical college; pursuing an associate's degree or professional certificate; or working toward a bachelor's, master's, or PhD at a state or private university.

SCHOLARSHIP MYTH 6: Scholarships are **only for U.S. citizens.**

FACT Many outside scholarships are available for non-U.S. citizens and recent immigrants. However, only U.S. citizens and eligible non-citizens may apply for federal student financial aid.

Pro Tip

Ask the financial aid offices at your top choice schools about any existing scholarship displacement policies. Most colleges have benevolent policies concerning the impact of outside scholarships on financial aid packages. Be sure to investigate these policies before making a final decision. If you negotiate any special arrangements, be sure to get them in writing.

SCHOLARSHIP MYTH 7: I must play on a competitive team in high school to qualify for **athletic scholarships**.

FACT: From golf to bowling and more, there are many opportunities for sports enthusiasts—whether or not a student plays on a school team. The simple enjoyment of a sport can help you qualify for certain outside scholarships.

SCHOLARSHIP MYTH 8: I can only apply to scholarships that **relate to my academic pursuits and career goals**.

FACT: Stating a specific career interest is only one of many paths to outside scholarships. Although you can find outside scholarships for virtually every field of study, there are also scholarships for students who are undecided. For example, we once worked with a student who used a history-related scholarship to pursue a biology degree.

CHECK this out!

DoSomething.org is an organization that offers numerous fun, off-beat, and wacky scholarships.

14

SCHOLARSHIP MYTH 9: I can win **only one scholarship**.

FACT: There is *no limit* to the number of outside scholarships you can win. None.

You now know that there are thousands upon thousands of outside scholarship opportunities. Some have a broad set of requirements and some have a narrow set. Your job is to *find the ones that apply to you*. Remember: you are working toward achieving your dreams!

Scholarship Opportunities

APPLE WWDC SCHOLARSHIP >>> For students age 13 and older who use their creativity and coding skills to build an app.

HARRY S. TRUMAN SCHOLARSHIP >>> Awarded to undergraduate students who fulfill numerous criteria related to public service.

DOODLE 4 GOOGLE >>> Students in K-12 submit original artwork for a chance to win scholarship money and for their doodle to appear on Google for a day.

In Chapter 2, we debunked many myths about scholarships.

☑ You feel confident about the variety of scholarship opportunities out there.

☑ You know the truth about outside scholarships, and do not let silly myths get in the way of your mission.

☑ You are taking steps toward achieving your dreams!

You're more than your GPA!!!

Chapter Three

Y O U :   A   P E R S O N A L   I N V E N T O R Y

Our next step is to tap the most valuable resource in this process: you. While the approach detailed in this book will *guide* your Money Mission, the personal details that are uniquely you will *drive* your mission and open doors to your specific opportunities.

Use the following prompts to help you brainstorm as you complete the Personal Search Engine List worksheet at the end of this chapter. Think about the many facets of your life; your answers will point you toward the right doors to knock on.

Start With the Basics

Take an inventory of yourself: your ethnicity and family heritage, religious affiliation, and physical characteristics. List the town, city, county, and state you live in. Describe your career goals, interests, and passions.

Call Out Your Accomplishments

Move on to your accomplishments—in and out of school, past and present. Where do you excel? What are you passionate about? Where do you work or volunteer? What are your most impressive achievements? List every single one of these items.

Catalog Your Body of Work

Some scholarships require you to submit additional materials with your application. During your high school career, every paper, project, poem, or multimedia presentation you've completed is worthy of submission, as long as it earned at least a B. Go ahead and dig out those past assignments and projects. These are your ready-to-go materials. Remember to include future assignments that meet the criteria.

Think Big

Don't overlook clubs and organizations when starting your research. In addition, you might be surprised to find scholarships that link to hobbies and interests. Do you play video games? There are scholarships for that! Do you recycle at home? There are scholarships that acknowledge young environmentalists. Are you a fashion maven? Use this interest. The possibilities are boundless!

Cast a Wide Net

As you create your list, you might find yourself excluding things that no longer seem relevant or important in your life. A word of caution: DON'T! You never know what might come in handy. Perhaps you once belonged to the Girl Scouts but have moved on to other activities. Your past involvement may qualify you for a

THINK BIG!

I Always WEAR Abercrombie + Fitch

→ LET ME run a SEARCH to SEE if A+F has a scholarship

A+F does offer a scholarship! IT REQUIRES applicants to take on ANTI-bullying PROJECTS

I also NEED to COMPLETE A COMMUNITY SERVICE project For SOCIAL STUDIES

→ I WIll DO a COMMUNITY SERVICE ProJect THAT Focuses on ANTI-Bullying

I got an A on My PROJect, and I have MATERIALs I can use For Abercrombie + Fitch's Scholarship APPLICATION! ←

scholarship. Or maybe you aced a medieval literature paper during your junior year. Even if you are set on a career in medicine, that assignment could net you an English scholarship.

Dig Deep

Even when you think your list is done, it probably isn't. Every item in your Personal Search Engine List is a starting point for capturing many more details about where you've come from and where you are going. Envision your goals and describe how they impact your family, your community, and the world. Use these specifics to target opportunities.

FROM JEAN'S FILES

I ONCE HAD THE CHANCE TO SPEAK TO A FUTURE NURSE FROM BROOKLYN, N.Y. THIS STUDENT KNEW WHAT SHE WANTED TO DO AND WAS GETTING STARTED ON HER MONEY MISSION. SHE LISTED "NURSE" FOR HER CAREER GOAL, BUT I FELT CERTAIN SHE HAD A MORE PRECISE VISION FOR HER FUTURE CAREER. I ASKED HER TO TELL ME MORE ABOUT THE SORT OF PEOPLE SHE'D LIKE TO HELP. SHE BARELY PAUSED BEFORE TELLING ME THAT SHE WANTED TO BECOME A NEONATAL NURSE IN NIGERIA, WHERE HER FAMILY IS FROM. BY ELABORATING ON THE DETAILS OF HER GOAL, HER LIST OF POSSIBILITIES TRIPLED! BE SURE YOU DO THIS TOO!

Enlist Your People

Ask your best friends and family members to help you with your list. The people who know you best are ideal assets to help you remember everything that's amazing and fabulous and wonderful about you.

Get Up Close and Personal

Ask your family to help you expand your personal details. Perhaps they will help you uncover a forgotten piece of family history, and open a door to another scholarship opportunity.

The goal of your Personal Search Engine List is to keep it growing. The more detailed you get about who you are, the more doors you will find.

Personal Search Engine List

Taking a personal inventory will help you identify your opportunities for outside scholarships. Use the area below to begin your Personal Search Engine List, and keep in mind that you will frequently amend this list.

YOU...THE BASICS	SEARCH

Ethnicity . . . .

Religious affiliation . . . .

Physical Characteristics. . . . .

. . . .

Geographic location (city, county, state) . . . .

. . . .

Career Goal(s) . . . .

. . . .

. . . .

Interests . . . .

. . . .

. . . .

Passions . . . .

. . . .

. . . .

. . . .

(EXAMPLE: MY GOAL IS TO TRAVEL WITH DOCTORS WITHOUT BORDERS!)

GPA/Test Scores . . . .
. . . .

Attendance . . . .
Clubs . . . .
. . . .
. . . .

Sports or Arts . . . .
. . . .
. . . .

Leadership or Mentoring . . . .
. . . .
. . . .

Community Service . . . .
. . . .
. . . .

Organizations . . . .
. . . .
. . . .

Jobs . . . .
. . . .

Other . . . .
. . . .

(EXAMPLE: I AM A FOUNDING MEMBER OF THE "SPEAK YOUR TRUTH" CLUB.)

Prepared Materials

Work smarter, not harder, and use your previous work for scholarship application submissions. Dig out the papers, projects, essays, and poems that earned you at least a B grade on school assignments, as well as any relevant material you have created for any clubs or organizations that you participate in.

WHAT DO YOU HAVE READY TO GO?   SEARCH

Papers . . . .
. . . .
. . . .
. . . .
. . . .
. . . .
. . . .

Projects . . . .
. . . .
. . . .
. . . .
. . . .
. . . .

(EXAMPLE: I WILL REVISIT THE PSA FILM PROJECT FROM DIGITAL MEDIA CLASS.)

Want to see a sample?
Check out www.connections101.com

Essays . . . .
. . . .
. . . .
. . . .
. . . .
. . . .
. . . .

Poems . . . .
. . . .
. . . .
. . . .
. . . .
. . . .
. . . .

Other . . . .
. . . .
. . . .
. . . .

In Chapter 3, you completed a
Personal Search Engine List.

☑ You have given thought to all of your
activities and achievements, which
will help inform your search for
scholarship opportunities.

☑ You understand that your Personal
Search Engine List is a work in progress,
which you will continue to add to.

Chapter Four

E X P A N D I N G   Y O U R   I N V E N T O R Y

Congratulations on your hard work! If you've noticed some gaps on your Personal Search Engine List, never fear! Your Money Mission always has more opportunities to uncover. Are you a straight-A student whose extracurricular activities are a bit thin? Maybe you are a community service superstar who has average grades. Whatever your current situation, it is not the end of your story. Every student has the ability to increase their Personal Search Engine List.

The Big 6

The majority of scholarships are awarded on the basis of grade point average, career goals, sports, clubs, leadership, and community service. We call these the Big 6. The best way to boost your Personal Search Engine List is to maximize what you have in your Big 6.

Community Service

CAREER GOALS

CLUBS

YOU

SPORTS

LEADERSHi

GPA

In Chapter 2 you learned that you can find scholarships beyond the major categories. Those are great, but the Big 6 are crucial. The truth is, more scholarship opportunities exist in these six categories than any others. Fortunately, you have the power to take action to improve your eligibility for scholarships, regardless of what you have accomplished prior to this point.

Most students will only apply to scholarships that perfectly match their Personal Search Engine List. For example, many B students only look for and apply to scholarships for B students.

Thankfully, you are on a Money Mission. You are going to take action to expand your lists and qualify for more. If you are that B student, you can step up your game and work toward becoming an A student. Go ahead and begin seeking scholarships for B+ and A students as you work to improve your current academic status.

No matter your circumstances, *you can choose* to put yourself in a better position to qualify for Big 6 scholarships.

How do you take action? The following Big 6 strategies will help you expand your Personal Search Engine List.

Increase Your GPA

Ask for extra credit projects, practice exams, and help sessions. Bringing up your average by a few points just might qualify you for a whole slew of scholarships you may have passed over before.

Be a Joiner

Identify your interests and join a related club. See what clubs your friends enjoy and consider joining them. If you cannot find a club you want to join, create a new one! Use your new memberships to impact your Personal Search Engine List.

Get Athletic

Whether you play a competitive sport or not, check out other athletic activities, like yoga, Zumba, bowling, or kickball. Participating may qualify you for a scholarship.

Serve Your Community

Volunteer for a community service project in your hometown. From youth to religious organizations, there are scores of charities that could benefit from your help—while you benefit too!

Lead the Way

Do more than just participate in a club or community service project. Run something, create something, and make something happen in your community. Be a leader! What will your leadership project be?

Explore Careers

Like many students, you might be unsure of your future career path. Try networking and exploration. Be an intern, job shadow a professional, or conduct research online and at your guidance office.

The Choice Is Yours

In your Money Mission and your life, *choice* is your most powerful tool. Push yourself and you will get more for yourself. You will become a stronger candidate and a stronger person. Keep up the good work; the sky is the limit!

GPA

At midterm, I had a solid B in French. For the remainder of the term, I took on every extra credit project and boosted my grade to a B+ by the end of the term!

COMMUNITY SERVICE

Collecting canned food from my neighbors for my synagogue's annual Thanksgiving food drive was a fun and rewarding way to serve my community.

LEADERSHIP

Our town park is one of my favorite places. When it was vandalized with graffiti over summer break, I called the police department and offered to organize a cleanup day.

SPORTS

I am not the most athletic person, but I decided to join the intramural soccer team. Even though I'm not a great player, I have so much fun.

CLUBS

I've always liked the school plays but am not much of an actor. I talked to a friend and learned that drama club always needs help painting sets, which I'm great at!

CAREER

A summer internship at my local town hall was a great way to explore my interests in law, civics, and local government.

THE BIG 6!!

Your Money Mission is underway!
You have made a commitment and
taken a personal inventory.

☑ You know that your ever-expanding
Personal Search Engine List
will connect you to scholarship
opportunities that are a fit for your past,
current, and future achievements.

☑ You are taking action in the
Big 6 to improve your candidacy
as an applicant.

Chapter Five

SETTING YOUR MONEY GOAL

Your next step is to start thinking about the number of scholarships you should apply for. As you might imagine, scholarships can be very competitive. Among the thousands of students we have met over the years, only a few have won every scholarship they applied to. With this in mind, you will need to increase your odds by applying for way more scholarships than you need. To meet your Money Mission goals, your strategy is to apply to as many scholarships as possible.

Think about your goals while reading the following statement:

On my Money Mission, my goal is to apply for __ scholarships.

Placing an actual number on your goal might seem daunting. Let's consider a great goal:

On my Money Mission, my goal is to apply for 100 scholarships a year.

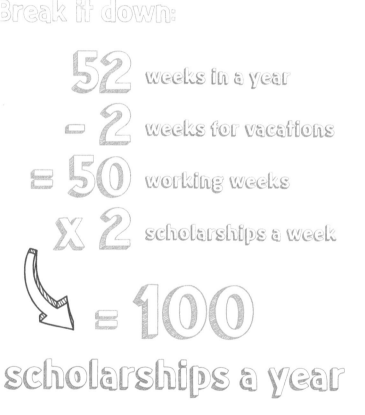

Break it down:

52 weeks in a year

- 2 weeks for vacations

= 50 working weeks

x 2 scholarships a week

= 100

scholarships a year

Wow! Applying to 100 scholarships is a wonderful goal! It may seem like a demanding mission, but when we BREAK IT DOWN, it becomes extremely doable. First, there are 52 weeks in a year. Go ahead and cross off two weeks for your birthday, favorite holiday, or vacation. Take your goal and divide it by 50 weeks. How does your goal sound now:

On my Money Mission, I pledge to apply to 2 scholarships every week.

Using the space below, factor your goal.

On my Money Mission, my goal is to apply for ＿＿ scholarships per year.

To break it down, that's ＿＿ per week.

I also will factor in breaks for:

Two per week is within your reach! Even when life throws you curve balls, you can manage this goal. By creating a manageable plan of action, your goal will become habit. Week by week and application by application, the task will become easier for you.

You'll feel more confident as you go. Stick to your minimum goal, at least at first. You don't want to burn out. Remember, your Money Mission is a marathon, not a sprint. Once you get more comfortable with the process, if you have the time, by all means, apply to a couple more.

The Matter of Money

Some students may think that they should only seek and apply for large scholarships. Those large scholarships are fantastic, if you

MISSED GOALS = MISSED OPPORTUNITIES

get them, but don't overlook smaller scholarship opportunities. *Every scholarship is worth applying for.* Don't focus on particular dollar amounts. As wonderful as big, juicy scholarships are, they are highly competitive. Realistically, you will not get everything you apply for. Therefore, it is just as important to go after the small scholarships as the large ones—as many as possible. In the end, recipients receive scholarships for a variety of amounts.

Cast a wide net. It's a strategy that will increase your odds of winning. After all, twenty $1,000 scholarships amount to the same as one $20,000 scholarship.

One Cool Scholarship

FLAVOR OF THE MONTH SCHOLARSHIP >>> Unigo offers a $1,500 Flavor of the Month Scholarship. Students 13 years of age or older are invited to write about their favorite ice cream flavor in 250 words or less. Check it out!

www.unigo.com/scholarships/our-scholarships/flavor-of-the-month-scholarship

Chapter Six

MAKING TIME TO MEET YOUR GOAL

Your life is filled with many demands. During the school year, you might have weeks and months when there is barely time to sleep. Countless obligations—school, church, sports, hobbies, friends, family—pull you in many directions. Additional responsibilities and activities are constantly slipping into your schedule.

Your weekly goal is a great step toward achieving your Money Mission, but how do you find time for it?

You've set a manageable weekly goal for yourself.

You must make it a priority that is ingrained in your life. You absolutely do not procrastinate, because doing so would hurt your Money Mission.

There are many ways you can carve out time to meet your goals. For example, you could:

- *Search for scholarships during every study hall.*
- *Apply to two weekly scholarships when your mom works late and you watch a younger sibling.*
- *Use bonus class time to print out scholarship applications.*

Find a clear path and make your Money Mission a priority. Do not allow obstacles to get in your way. After all, what is more important than your dreams and your future? When you make smart choices about managing time, you will meet your application goals and improve your chances for more money.

Even if you are the busiest student on the planet, you can achieve your goals. Take a look at this very full schedule:

MONDAY

7:15-11:40	Classes
11:45-12:30	Lunch - Hang with Kim, plan clothing drive for Operation Outreach Club
12:35-2:10	Classes
2:15-5:00	Soccer practice
5:30-8:00	Write essay for AP history assignment
8:00-10:00	Homework for rest of classes
10:00-11:00	Chat with friends

No doubt about it, this is a packed schedule. If your days look like this, the idea of adding one more thing may feel positively exhausting. But remember your mission and think bigger! Somewhere in this day there are 30 minutes to spare.

A few modifications, and...

12:20-12:30
Leave early. Online scholarship search. Found 3 related to US history!

5:15-5:25
Update Personal Search Engine List and download scholarship applications while grabbing a quick bite at home.

MONDAY

7:15-11:40	Classes
11:45-~~12:30~~	lunch – Hang with Kim, plan clothing drive for Operation Outreach Club
12:35-2:10	Classes
2:15-5:00	Soccer practice
~~5:30~~-8:00	Write essay for AP history assignment
8:00-10:00	Homework for rest of classes
~~10:00~~-11:00	Chat with friends

10:05-10:15
Fill out US history scholarship application. Adjust my homework essay from tonight to fit the application essay requirement. Set phone reminder to submit it tomorrow.

This student carved out three 10-minute slots in an already packed day. It just goes to show you, when you implement time management strategies, your goals stay within reach. Remember, your Money Mission will help you build the life of your dreams!

Customize Your Schedule

No two students follow the same schedule when it comes to their Money Missions. One student may only have lunch and study hall for working on their goals. Another student might maximize a 30-minute bus ride each morning.

Each day will be different too, and can be adjusted according to your commitments. Some days you'll do what you need to do in a single session, and other days you'll need to break it into two or three chunks.

There will be instances when you need to devote extra time to application materials. Try to optimize your time by dedicating an uninterrupted hour to your mission. After all, if you received a $100 scholarship for spending just one hour on an essay, wouldn't that be worth your time?

Once you get comfortable with the process, try to add some bonus time to your schedule. An extra 10 minutes here and there could help you search and apply for more opportunities.

It is possible for you to meet all of your obligations *and* work on your Money Mission!

This is a MUST if I want The MONEY!

Strategies for Maximizing Your Time

If you have 10 minutes...

- Ask your parents if their employer offers any scholarships to children of employees.

- Print an application and begin to fill it out.

- Submit a batch of completed applications.

If you have 30 minutes...

- Complete an especially long application.

- Interview a grandparent about family history.

- Revise an essay of yours to fit a new scholarship.

If you have an hour...

- Copy down scholarship information while you're at a favorite hangout spot.

- Answer essay questions.

- Hunt for scholarships with a friend. Share notes and stay motivated together.

43

FROM JEAN'S FILES

"JEAN, YOU DON'T UNDERSTAND. I AM BUSIER THAN MOST STUDENTS." AFTER ONE OF MY TALKS, A SENIOR APPROACHED ME WITH THIS DILEMMA. AS WE CHATTED, I LEARNED THAT THE STUDENT HAD BEEN WORKING EXTRA HOURS AT HER PART-TIME JOB TO HELP PAY THE BILLS WHILE HER MOTHER WAS UNEMPLOYED. AND ON TOP OF THAT, THE STUDENT HAD AN INFANT SON TO CARE FOR. HER SCHEDULE WAS FULL TO BURSTING.

I ADVISED HER TO FIND 10 MINUTES, THREE TIMES A WEEK. EVERYONE CAN DO THIS! HEARING THIS, SHE IMAGINED NEW POSSIBILITIES. AFTER SOME QUICK THINKING, SHE DECIDED THAT SHE WOULD ARRIVE AT SCHOOL 10 MINUTES EARLY (OR STAY 10 MINUTES LATE) EVERY TUESDAY, WEDNESDAY, AND THURSDAY, AND USE A SCHOOL COMPUTER TO WORK ON HER MONEY MISSION.

OVER THE COURSE OF HER SENIOR YEAR, SHE APPLIED TO ALMOST 200 SCHOLARSHIPS. SHE DIDN'T WIN THEM ALL, BUT SHE RECEIVED ABOUT $80,000 IN SCHOLARSHIPS. SHE WAS ABLE TO PAY IN FULL FOR COLLEGE AND AFFORD CHILDCARE FOR HER SON. SHE PRIORITIZED HER FUTURE, MAXIMIZED HER TIME, AND WON BIG!

Tweet Little Scholarships

Several companies, such as Kentucky Fried Chicken, have awarded scholarships based on creative tweets. Business experts predict that this trend will only increase as popular brands seek positive publicity.

You have a time management strategy to help you achieve your goals.

Chapter Seven

BEGIN LOCALLY

You are ready to begin your search! To stay on track, you will need to use your time efficiently. Unnecessary busywork is not your friend! So, where do you begin?

Ask Your Family

Your search begins with your family—your parents, aunts and uncles, grandparents, and other close relatives. Make a list of every one of your relatives and make a point to connect with each

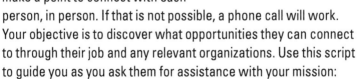

person, in person. If that is not possible, a phone call will work. Your objective is to discover what opportunities they can connect to through their job and any relevant organizations. Use this script to guide you as you ask them for assistance with your mission:

"You won't believe it, but I'm graduating from high school in [month/year]. Going to college is an important step toward achieving my future dreams. Those dreams definitely do *not* include accruing massive student loan debt, so I'm on a mission to find as many scholarships as possible to defray college costs. I'm reaching out to you to see if you would ask your employer if the company offers any scholarship opportunities for family members. I'd also love it if you'd look into scholarships offered by any organizations you are involved with. It only takes a minute for you to ask, but any information you find would be very valuable to me."

In many cases, your family members will not have heard of any particular scholarships. Be prepared for them to casually dismiss your inquiry. Their quick answer may be, "I'd love to help, but I've never heard of any scholarships."

If this is the case, you will respectfully respond, "I'd really appreciate it if you'd double check, just in case there is." If someone in your family isn't sure where to look, suggest that they check with human resources or a director.

It Pays To Ask

Bryce attended church every Sunday and was active in the high school youth group. During his local scholarship search, he asked if the church had a scholarship for young members. It didn't. But the story doesn't end there. The congregation decided to start a new scholarship and took up a special collection to fund it. Although any high school student at the church could apply, Bryce was pleased that his inquiry led to a new opportunity.

Ask Around Town

After your family, think locally. Find out what your community offers. There are many businesses and organizations that would like to support ambitious young people in your community. After that, you'll broaden your search to your county, and finally your state. Only after you have tapped out local and regional opportunities will you move on to national and international scholarships.

Why does it matter? Statistically, you have a much better chance of winning local scholarships because they attract a smaller pool of applicants. Let's compare two examples:

Scholarship A: A national retailer is offering a $1,000 raffle to one lucky student. It takes two minutes to fill out and submit the online form. There are 5,000 applicants.

Scholarship B: Your local Elks Lodge offers a $500 community service scholarship. Applicants must attend the local high school and submit a 300-word essay. Twenty students apply.

By all means, apply to both of them! But if you are tempted to pass on the smaller, local scholarship, please reconsider. Your likelihood of being awarded that scholarship is 1 in 20, versus the national prize, which has much longer odds of 1 to 5,000. The local scholarship might take a bit more work, but it is absolutely worth your time.

1 in 20!!!

49

The success of your mission requires you to be vigilant about looking for scholarship opportunities. Any place that you frequent should now be considered a potential scholarship resource: restaurants, retail stores, cultural centers, the library, your church, and any other places you regularly visit. Go ahead and visit websites of local establishments, but don't forget the power of making a personal connection. When you pick up your carry out order later this week, ask if the owner offers any scholarships to local students. When your parents hire contractors or other service providers, ask those folks too.

FROM JEAN'S FILES

I NEEDED MONEY FOR COLLEGE TOO! WHEN I WAS IN HIGH SCHOOL, MY DAD WORKED IN CONSTRUCTION AND HAD BEEN A UNION MEMBER FOR OVER 20 YEARS. I ASKED HIM IF THERE WAS ANY CHANCE HIS CONSTRUCTION UNION OFFERED A SCHOLARSHIP, BUT HE SAID, "WE DON'T HAVE ANYTHING LIKE THAT. AFTER ALL MY YEARS WITH THE COMPANY, IF THERE WAS A SCHOLARSHIP, I WOULD HAVE HEARD OF IT."

I PRESSED, "WELL DAD, COULD YOU JUST ASK?" AGAIN, HE INSISTED THAT HE WOULD HAVE KNOWN ABOUT ANY SCHOLARSHIPS. AT THAT POINT, I URGED HIM TO PLEASE JUST ASK. THANKFULLY HE RELENTED AND WAS SURPRISED TO LEARN THAT HIS CONSTRUCTION UNION OFFERED A $3,500 SCHOLARSHIP. I APPLIED AND GOT IT! I WAS THANKFUL, AND SO WAS MY DAD!

If you've ever been involved with Boy Scouts, Girl Scouts, Boys and Girls Club, or the YMCA/YWCA, those and many other youth groups offer scholarship opportunities as well.

Visit your local chamber of commerce and ask for a copy of their member list. Add those businesses to your search. Find out if your chamber of commerce awards scholarships on behalf of its members.

Finally, be sure to reach out to local branches of civic, fraternal, service, and veterans organizations such as American Legion, Elks, Freemasons, Junior League, Kiwanis, Knights of Columbus, League of Women Voters, Odd Fellows, Rotary International, Veterans of Foreign Wars, as well as community foundations and other relevant groups. Search locally and win!

Your Money Mission is a monumental task. Scholarship money is out there, but you must work to find it. Keep asking! Follow up with your leads in a timely fashion, and always remember to express your gratitude for any assistance you receive.

You have launched an ambitious scholarship search that begins locally.

Chapter Eight

SCHOOL RESOURCES

Myriad opportunities abound in your community, but perhaps
you noticed a critical omission: your school. Because you spend
more time here than anywhere else, you have a dynamic network
that is ready to tap. The following guidelines highlight key areas
for you to investigate, to ensure that you fully use the scholarship
resources available at your school.

Visit Your Guidance Office

Make yourself a weekly visitor in the college guidance office.
Always ask about any new scholarship information that has been
received. When you become a regular visitor, you are less likely to
miss out on an opportunity, and it's more likely that the counselors
will inform you of new opportunities. Your proactive approach will
help you gain better results. DON'T PLAY THE WAITING GAME!

Strengthen Your Existing Network

Make a list of the school personnel who know you best—ideally 5 individuals. This may include coaches, teachers, administrators, staff members, or other important people. Make a special effort to nurture your relationship with each individual, and ask them to help you with your Money Mission. They may be aware of scholarship opportunities that you overlooked or were unaware of. Remember to ask them to let you know about any new scholarships they come across.

Grow Your Network

Additionally, identify the people—usually teachers, administrators, or parents—on the committees of school-sponsored scholarships. Connect with a committee member, and let that person know you are interested in the scholarship. Ask them what traits an ideal candidate should possess, as well as how you can increase your likelihood of receiving that particular scholarship.

Talk to Recent Winners

Using a program from the most recent awards ceremony (check with your guidance office for a copy), look at the list of scholarship winners. Reach out to recipients and ask them to share insights on how they found scholarships and what they did to set themselves apart from other applicants. Ask them if they would consider sharing a list of scholarships that you could apply to.

Be a Leader

If your club doesn't offer a scholarship, be a leader! Coordinate a car wash, a pancake breakfast, or some other fundraiser. A new scholarship is one way club members could choose to use the funds. No matter the outcome, the leadership experience will be a great asset for you to mention on an application or essay.

Stay Organized

As you search, make sure to stick to the schedule that you designed in Chapter 6. Note deadlines on your Application Timeline (see Chapter 10). Reference your Personal Search Engine List for ready-to-go materials that can be used for applications. Take notes throughout the process. Ask questions. Advocate for yourself and always be prepared to make a good impression to a potential lead.

FROM JEAN'S FILES

I ONCE LEARNED OF A $20,000 ALUMNA-SPONSORED SCHOLARSHIP AT A SCHOOL I HAD JUST SPOKEN AT. IT WAS A BIG SCHOOL—ABOUT 3,000 STUDENTS—SO I ASSUMED THE APPLICANT POOL WOULD BE LARGE. BUT WHEN I ASKED A GUIDANCE COUNSELOR ABOUT IT, HER ANSWER ALMOST KNOCKED ME OVER. "SIX, I HAVE SIX APPLICATIONS ON MY DESK," SHE SAID. THOSE SIX STUDENTS WERE VERY LUCKY TO HAVE THE ODDS SO HUGELY IN THEIR FAVOR. BUT SHOULDN'T MORE STUDENTS HAVE APPLIED? OF COURSE THEY SHOULD HAVE. WHEN I ASKED STUDENTS AT THAT SCHOOL WHY THEY HADN'T APPLIED, THEY SAID THEY DIDN'T KNOW ABOUT IT.

AS A STUDENT ON A MONEY MISSION YOU WOULD HAVE CERTAINLY KNOWN ABOUT IT, BECAUSE YOU ARE MAKING IT YOUR BUSINESS TO KNOW ABOUT IT.

You are networking at your
school, with your family, and
in your community.

☑ Your local search is on—
and it's hot!

Chapter Nine

TAKING YOUR SEARCH NATIONAL

Once you've exhausted your local options, it's time to expand your search and look nationally. As you might guess, typing "scholarship" into your browser's search engine might not be the best use of your carefully scheduled time. Wouldn't it be wonderful if there were a comprehensive list of scholarships?

Scholarship Books

Your local library contains a valuable resource: knowledgeable librarians who can help you search for relevant resources such as the most current editions of scholarship books. These books are published annually and contain indexes that you can match to your Personal Search Engine List. Once you have one in hand, flip to the index and get to work. It's easy and quick! Using these books assures you that the information is active for the current year. In 30 minutes or less,

I have 30 MINUTES

(EXAMPLE: I WILL REPURPOSE THE POEM I WROTE AT SUMMER CAMP LAST YEAR)

you can jot down dozens of scholarships that match your Personal Search Engine List. You could also check your school library or guidance office for these resources. You might also find them at your favorite book store, but be sure to ask for permission before you begin using their copy for your personal reference.

Does this strategy sound impossibly easy or too good to be true? Let's compare two scenarios:

Paul searches for soccer scholarships on the internet, and subsequently spends three hours sifting through 40 websites. Several links lead to expired or irrelevant information, contain vague references that require more searching, or require Paul to create an account.

Elizabeth opens the index of a scholarship book, finds soccer scholarships, and spends 20 minutes copying down useful information.

What do you think now? Using your time effectively will help you meet your weekly application goals. Efficiency matters!

Stack the Odds in Your Favor

Many scholarship books contain useful statistics, such as how many students applied and how many were awarded. Use this data to prioritize the scholarships you apply to. For example:

Soccer Scholarship #1 had 382 applicants last year.

Soccer Scholarship #2 had 93 applicants last year.

If each scholarship awarded one winner, #2 has better odds, and you should therefore apply to that option. However, if you learn that #1 awarded nine scholarships and #2 awarded just one, then choose #1 with its better odds. Doing the math will help you prioritize your options. Give top priority to the scholarships that offer the best probability. Later, you can move on to the longer shots. Making smart choices economizes your time and gives you the best chances for success!

As you pursue your Money Mission, choose the opportunities that offer the best odds.

Go Beyond Your List

Once you have exhausted your Personal Search Engine List, begin looking for peripheral opportunities. Scan scholarship indexes several more times. Note scholarships that interest you. Your numbers game bursts with potential when you take advantage of scholarship books.

During your secondary scan, you'll find general scholarships to which any student can apply. In addition, you might encounter opportunities that spark a new idea. Maybe you'll stumble upon a history scholarship. Although that subject may not have been on your Personal Search Engine List, when you see the scholarship you might remember earning an A on a history essay during your sophomore year. Bam! There's another one on your list. As you see, taking the time to look will positively impact your numbers game.

Beyond this, there are hundreds of scholarships that don't fit into traditional categories. Some of them are so unusual that you would never think to look for them. For instance:

$2,500 for taking a picture of your school lunch

$2,000 for writing about how you'd survive a zombie apocalypse

As you continue to brainstorm and research, the numbers game becomes increasingly easier. Using scholarship books is an efficient and effective strategy that delivers results!

Don't Forget the Future

Using scholarship books is a great strategy for an older student—whether you are pursuing an advanced degree or are a nontraditional student—as scholarship websites are typically geared toward high school students. If your career path necessitates graduate school, make a note of applicable scholarships for future reference. Your Money Mission does not stop on high school graduation day.

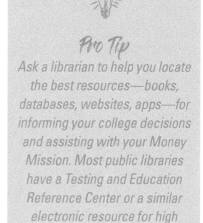

Pro Tip

Ask a librarian to help you locate the best resources—books, databases, websites, apps—for informing your college decisions and assisting with your Money Mission. Most public libraries have a Testing and Education Reference Center or a similar electronic resource for high school students.

Wacky
Scholarship

Save the Frogs!
Art Contest

Open to all ages.
Requirement: Create frog artwork.
$100
www.savethefrogs.com/art

More Time ⟹

Meeting Your Application Goals ⟹

Winning the Numbers Game!

You are using scholarship
books to efficiently search for
national scholarships.

Chapter Ten

CREATING AN APPLICATION TIMELINE

You need a strategy for managing deadlines. Creating and maintaining an Application Timeline is a practical way to stay on track and meet your goals.

Keep It Organized

In order to avoid the potential pitfalls that may accompany your piles of options, you must organize your applications *as you find them*. After all, the last thing that you want is to miss a deadline. Creating a simple system will make organizing a snap.

First, everything must be filed. You may choose to organize your applications in physical files or on your computer (or some of both, depending on the applications). Either way, you'll need to create a folder for each month and organize applications chronologically within each folder.

Secondly, you'll need to keep a calendar. Whether you keep a calendar on your smartphone or go old school and maintain a paper calendar, you'll need to chart deadlines. Using a calendar to organize your Application Timeline will help you stay on top of individual requirements—such as following up on the letter of recommendation that you requested—and meet every deadline.

Taking basic steps to map out your deadlines creates a clear path for you to follow. When you stick to your Application Timeline, you will stay on track and advance your Money Mission goals.

Stay Ahead

Application due dates are a logical way to organize your schedule, but as you look ahead to each week or month, remember:

- *Stack your odds by giving priority to local scholarships over national scholarships.*

- *Highlight the scholarships that will require more of your time. Start those applications early.*

- *Allow plenty of time to the wonderful people who are writing letters on your behalf, and set a goal to collect letters two weeks before the application due date. This strategy allows for some wiggle room if your people need more time.*

- *Focus on submitting applications early. Do not wait until the last minute.*

- *Keep your weekly goals in mind, and continue to search for more opportunities.*

These strategies will help you meet your deadlines. As long as you do the work to stay on track, your Money Mission is unstoppable! Keep going, you're doing great! The life of your dreams is attainable!

Plan your month, Then work your plan!

Month at a Glance

To achieve a goal of submitting two scholarship applications per week, you'll need to map out requirements in your weekly timeline. The following example shows how you could complete eight applications in four weeks.

Mom's union scholarship for family members

REQUIRED: TEACHER RECOMMENDATION LETTER

Week 1 request recommendation letter from a teacher
Week 2 remind teacher about recommendation letter
Week 3 pick up recommendation letter, complete and
submit application

Odds: **EXCELLENT** *– limited to employee family members*

Local chamber of commerce scholarship

REQUIRED: 1,500 WORD ESSAY

Week 2 write first draft
Week 3 have someone proofread it
Week 4 finalize essay, complete and submit application

Odds: **VERY GOOD** *– fewer students willing to write essays; limited to local students*

Local community service scholarship

REQUIRED: 500 WORD ESSAY

Week 2   write first draft
Week 3   have someone proofread it
Week 4   finalize essay, complete and submit application

Odds: **GOOD** *– shorter essay; limited to local students*

National community service scholarship

REQUIRED: PHOTOS FROM RECENT COMMUNITY SERVICE PROJECT

Week 2   compile some great photos, complete and
             submit application

Odds: **FAIR** *– some work required; huge pool of eligible applicants*

National creativity scholarship

REQUIRED: 160 CHARACTER MESSAGE POSTED TO SPONSORING
COMPANY'S SOCIAL MEDIA PAGE

Week 1   write and post your 160 character message

Odds: **LONG SHOT** *– easy requirement; huge pool of applicants*

Statewide poetry competition scholarship

REQUIRED: NON–PUBLISHED ORIGINAL POEM

Week 1   dig out a poem from ready-to-go materials and
             submit with application

Odds: **FAIR** *– some work required; many eligible students*

National video contest scholarship

REQUIRED: VIDEO THAT MOTIVATES VIEWERS TO TAKE ACTION

Week 1 retrieve video from ready-to-go materials
(from 9th grade assignment)

Week 2 complete application, attach video, submit

Odds: **GOOD** *– requires moderate work; fewer students willing
to do work*

National essay scholarship

REQUIRED: 3–5 PAGE ESSAY ABOUT PATRIOTISM

Week 1 dig out 10-page paper from ready-to-go
materials (from 10th grade assignment)

Week 2 condense and redraft paper to focus on
patriotism; have someone proofread it

Week 3 make final changes, complete and
submit application

Odds: **GOOD** *– requires moderate work; fewer willing to write essays*

STACK The Dollars

You've tapped your local resources—your family, your community, and your school—and you've taken your search national by using scholarship books.

Chapter Eleven

CONDUCTING AN ONLINE SEARCH

The next step in your mission is to conduct an online search that continues to align with your time management strategies and weekly goals. As you begin, be sure to visit the sites listed on "Jean's Top 10" (page 73). You'll find that some resources are general and others are specific to interests or personal characteristics. With that in mind, be sure to explore numerous sites. Each site focuses on different opportunities, so it's important to visit many in order to maximize your results. You are always playing the numbers game during your Money Mission.

Scholarship websites require you to complete a survey about your personal characteristics, interests, and objectives. Your answers help scholarships find you! Sifting through the results (generally delivered by email) will require extra time, so remember your time management strategies and don't allow yourself to get bogged down with useless information.

Scholarship websites provide filtering service at no cost because they share registration information with groups that target college students. In other words, you will get spam. Most of what you find in your junk folder will be related to summer programs, degree programs, student loan companies, career recruiting, etc. That said, check your spam folder periodically for relevant scholarship information. You don't want to miss out on a great opportunity.

Pro Tip

If you are concerned about getting spam at your primary email, create a special email account exclusively for scholarship searching.

Maintain Your Momentum

Putting these tried-and-true strategies into action will help you stay on track as you go online with your Money Mission:

MATCH YOUR LIST: Match your Personal Search Engine List categories to those listed on scholarship websites and to the results you receive via email.

WORK WITH A FRIEND: Join forces with a friend as you both search for scholarships online. Pledge to share opportunities with one another. Scholarships that aren't a good fit for you could be perfect for your friend… and vice versa.

"The community service section on my Personal Search Engine List was a little empty. But then I visited dosomething.org and discovered that if I send a birthday card to a homeless child, I would be entered to win a $5,000 scholarship. This opportunity helped me get ahead in the numbers game, and it felt nice to do something kind. What a win-win!"

—Nina O., 11th Grade Student

USE SOCIAL NETWORKING: Keep your Money Mission fresh in the minds of your family and friends by making regular posts on social media about your journey. One week you might post a selfie taken in the library with a scholarship book. The next week you may share an infograph about college costs. Another time you might share your latest scholarship success. Remind your network to tell you about any scholarship opportunities they come across.

TAKE ADVANTAGE OF PORTABLE INFO: Having scholarship information delivered to your inbox means you can search anywhere! Search on the bus, between classes, or anywhere else you can find a few minutes!

PRIORITIZE: As with your local and national searches, remember to research the number of previous applicants and give priority to those with the best odds.

STAY ORGANIZED: Remember to organize your search within a weekly schedule that is *convenient to you.*

EXPAND YOUR LIST: Our scholarship website list contains abundant possibilities for you. As with searching scholarship books, allow the information you encounter to spark new ideas for your Personal Search Engine List. Remember to update your list with new experiences, awards, honors, projects, and activities.

Scholarship Scams

During the course of your search, you may encounter a scam. Trust your instincts and be cautious of scholarships that don't feel right, contain suspicious requirements, or make unusual guarantees.

NEVER PAY A FEE OR SEND MONEY to apply for a scholarship. Applying for scholarships should never cost more than the price of a stamp. If you encounter a scholarship that requires a processing or application fee, it is probably a scam. You should not have to pay money to get money.

NEVER GIVE OUT PERSONAL INFORMATION such as your social security number, bank account number, or credit card information to outside scholarship providers.

If you suspect that you've found a scam, ask your school counselor take a look at it. If it is a scam, you can report it to the National Fraud Information Center.

FROM JEAN'S FILES

THERE AREN'T WORDS FOR HOW MUCH I LOVE FINAID.ORG! IT IS QUITE POSSIBLY THE MOST COMPREHENSIVE SOURCE OF STUDENT FINANCIAL AID INFORMATION. BEST OF ALL, IT'S FREE TO USE, ADVERTISES OPPORTUNITIES WITHOUT MARKETING STUDENT INFORMATION TO OTHER COMPANIES, AND LINKS TO SCHOLARSHIPS FOR STUDENTS OF ALL AGES. THE DOWNSIDE IS THAT YOU'LL HAVE TO SIFT THROUGH LONG LISTS OF SCHOLARSHIPS WITHOUT THE AID OF FILTERS. REGARDLESS, IT IS A GREAT TOOL FOR FINDING SCHOLARSHIPS.

Jean's Top 10

Recommended Scholarship Websites

www.cappex.com/scholarships

www.chegg.com

www.dosomething.org

www.fastweb.com

www.nextstudent.com

www.scholarships4students.com

www.scholarshippoints.com

www.studentscholarships.org

www.supercollege.com

www.unigo.com

**For more scholarship websites
and resources visit
www.connections101.com**

You possess the resources to conduct a productive online scholarship search.

Your Money Mission has reached a point at which the possibilities awaiting you are seemingly endless.

Chapter Twelve

W R I T I N G   W I N N I N G   E S S A Y S

As you work toward your goals, sooner or later you will encounter an application requiring an essay. You have a busy schedule, and it's understandable that you might be reluctant to devote valuable time to essay writing. But applications with essay requirements may draw a smaller pool of applicants, which can help you win big.

Essays are a crucial component of many scholarship applications. A thoughtfully composed and well-written essay will stand out to the application committee. Illuminate your personal message by implementing strategies that will make your essays powerful and precise.

Why Me?

An effective essay will explain *why* the committee should select you. When you contemplate the future of your dreams, what impact do you wish to make in the world? How do you plan to use your education to change your life and impact others?

My "why me" Statement

_____

_____

_____

_____

_____

_____

Take a few days to think about these questions, and write a one or two sentence "why me" statement in the space above.

Once you have your "why me" statement, you'll be able to start writing winning essays. As you knock out essays, keep your statement in mind and be sure that each essay supports your statement from beginning to end.

Writing Essays That Shine

When you write an essay, your objective is to give the committee a sense of the real you. Convey the qualities that make you unique. Tell the story. Use an experience to show your leadership skills or how you faced adversity. It's okay if your story isn't dramatic; it isn't necessary to have endured hardship to win scholarships.

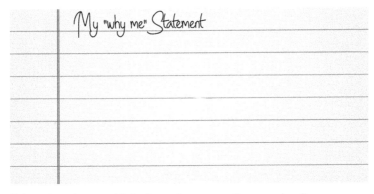

Pro Tip

Write your essays in your own true voice. Flowery language and heavy thesaurus use may detract from your message.

Scholarship committees read through countless essays before selecting a winner. You want yours to shine among the masses. Make sure your essay captures readers' attention from beginning to end.

START STRONG. A strong essay begins with an introductory paragraph that shows that you fully grasp the essay question. Your "why me" statement should also be incorporated as a compelling argument for why you *deserve* to receive the scholarship.

CAPTURE THEIR ATTENTION. When you write your story in a narrative style, you invite the reader to relive the memory with you. Don't simply state the information: "My brother's accident changed my life forever." Instead, *tell the story*: "I'll never forget the moment I answered the phone. It was my mom calling with a year's worth of bad news. My brother had been injured in a biking accident, and life as we knew it would change forever."

HOLD THEIR ATTENTION. Use details! Include sensory descriptors: taste, sight, sound, feeling. These details help readers connect with your experience throughout the essay.

Brainstorming 101: A field trip is an excellent experience to include in an essay. Perhaps a recent class trip to the capital took you to some interesting sites and piqued your interest in government. Such an experience would be a great topic for an essay for a social science scholarship. And don't forget to add it to your Personal Search Engine List. But you already knew that, right? You are on a Money Mission!

LEAVE A LASTING IMPRESSION. Use the conclusion of your essay to recap your response to the essay question. Additionally, leave the reader with a memorable thought that demonstrates "why you" should be awarded the scholarship.

FIND AN EDITOR. No matter how good your essays are, your message can be easily derailed by distracting typos, grammatical errors, or sentences that don't make sense. Enlist the help of a teacher, a counselor, the writing center, or other school resource to proofread your essay.

Continue to update your Personal Search Engine List.

YOU...THE BASICS

SEARCH

ACCOMPLISHMENTS AND EXTRACURRICULARS

SEARCH

WHAT DO YOU HAVE READY TO GO?

SEARCH

Additionally, be sure someone reviews the content and message of your essay. Ask the reviewer if the essay makes sense and if they found any gaps or holes in your storytelling. Once your essay is in the hands of the committee members, you want to make certain that it makes an excellent impression.

In the end, it is impossible to predict which essay will appeal to a scholarship committee. The best you can do is to write a fabulous essay that demonstrates why you deserve their money for your education. Commit to writing strong essays as a key component of your Money Mission!

FROM JEAN'S FILES

I OFTEN HEAR FROM STUDENTS AFTER THEY HAVE COMPLETED THEIR MONEY MISSION. ONE SUCH STUDENT, AN ASPIRING TEACHER, WON A BOATLOAD OF MONEY. WHEN I ASKED HER TO ELABORATE ON THE KEY TO HER SUCCESS, SHE EXPLAINED THAT SHE HAD REALLY FOCUSED ON HER "WHY ME" STATEMENT, WHICH WAS:

"IF YOUR ORGANIZATION GRANTS ME THIS SCHOLARSHIP MONEY, I'D LIKE YOU TO KNOW THAT MY GOAL IS TO GO BEYOND TEACHING. MY GOAL IS TO BECOME A PRINCIPAL OR SUPERINTENDENT ONE DAY. I WANT THE OPPORTUNITY TO IMPACT AND INSPIRE NOT JUST HUNDREDS OF STUDENTS, BUT THOUSANDS."

HER GOALS REACHED THE SCHOLARSHIP COMMITTEES THROUGH HER STRONG AND CLEAR "WHY ME" STATEMENT, AND IT PERSUADED THEM TO CHOOSE HER, WHICH KEPT HER MONEY MISSION STRONG!

You have made a commitment to write strong essays as a key component in your Money Mission.

You know that the potential payoff for writing great essays makes them totally worth your time.

Chapter Thirteen

WORKING SMARTER WITH ESSAYS

You have many scholarships to apply to and your life is so busy. How are you going to get to all of the essays? Never fear! You can keep your Money Mission moving and meet your application goals by reusing essays that you have already written.

Proceed With Care

Reusing a previously written essay is a great way to maximize your time. However, you must not be careless. There's a fundamental difference between reusing a story and reusing an essay. Sloppy mistakes are bound to occur if you simply copy and paste an old essay into a new one. For example, you might inadvertently address the wrong college, scholarship, or committee. Or you might forget to change the essay from a college application focus to a scholarship focus.

Such an embarrassing oversight is guaranteed to land your application directly into the trash. Students on a Money Mission strive to get their applications on top of the pile!

Revisiting Essays

When you recycle a previously written essay, you will need to tweak it so that it perfectly addresses the prompt. For example, you once wrote an essay responding to this prompt:

CHOOSE AN EXPERIENCE FROM YOUR LIFE AND EXPLAIN HOW IT HAS INFLUENCED WHO YOU ARE TODAY.

In this scenario, you wrote an essay that focuses on how your scout troop persevered in order to win a regional competition. You focused on positive actions and results.

> *I credit my leadership skills to the summer of the Great Survival Competition. My scout troop practiced every weekend....*

You are now faced with an essay that asks you to detail a failure. Read the new essay prompt carefully:

RECOUNT AN INCIDENT WHEN YOU FACED FAILURE AND DESCRIBE WHAT YOU LEARNED FROM IT.

You want to repurpose your scouting essay, but there is a major difference between the two essay topics. You need to tweak your original message and make some edits.

> *My scout troop lost the Great Survival Competition for four consecutive years. But this year, we put our heads together and committed to practicing harder than ever before. Our teamwork paid off, and we not only overcame previous defeats, but became a closer group. As patrol leader, my leadership skills grew tremendously from that experience.*

Personal Statement Essays

There are three common essay subjects that will come up over and over on scholarship (and college) applications. Work smarter, not harder!

Who is a person who has influenced your life and why?

What career path are you choosing to pursue and why?

What obstacle have you overcome and how has it made you who you are today?

As you can see, if the situation fits, you can use the same story to answer both questions. Just make certain that you tailor each essay to align with the specific theme.

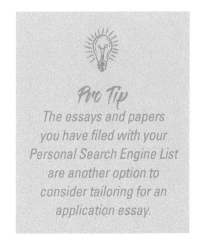

Recycling College Application Essays

You can even reuse a college application essay for a scholarship essay. Think of it this way: you've already invested time and energy by writing one essay. Double its impact by using it again. Naturally, the inverse is true as well. You can adapt a scholarship application essay to use on a college application.

Essays are an essential part of your Money Mission. You need them to apply for college and to get money to pay for it. Do the work, but use your time wisely. After all, you want your application to rise to the top of the pile.

Essay Checklist

Use this checklist with every essay that you prepare, whether it is a new essay or has been recycled. For further information on these points, refer to Chapter 12.

- My essay clearly states why I should get the scholarship money.

- My uniqueness stands out.

- My introduction shows that I understand the essay prompt or question.

- My essay uses descriptive and narrative language to catch the attention of the scholarship committee.

- My essay is filled with details designed to hold the attention of the scholarship committee.

- My strong conclusion will leave a lasting impression.

- My essay is free of spelling and grammatical errors.

- My essay clearly communicates its message.

You have many strategies to economize your time when it comes to writing essays.

Your Money Mission is in full swing!

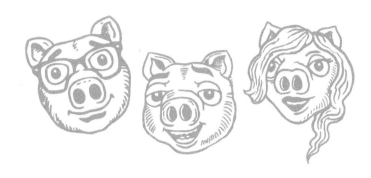

Chapter Fourteen

SCHOLARSHIP CLUBS

Did you know that you can fortify your Money Mission by working with other students? A scholarship club is a brilliant strategy to keep your mission going full throttle. When club members share opportunities, it revs up your mission and frees time for more scholarships.

You might question whether it's a smart strategy to share scholarship opportunities with people you will likely compete against. It's natural to feel competitive, and it's always up to you to decide what you want to share. But by joining forces, you'll have access to more scholarships than you would otherwise. Sharing is a small trade-off for what you'll get in the end. And when your peers win money, it just might help you stay motivated.

Creating a Scholarship Club

Recruit a few school friends to start your club. Work together to create a **mission statement** to help the group stay on track.

Get the word out. Make posters, set up a table, take advantage of school email blasts. Recruit as many members as possible, and be sure to open the group to all grade levels. Don't forget to incorporate the mission statement into your advertising.

Decide on a meeting time. Your group should meet regularly. After school is a great time to meet, but you could also meet during study hall, lunchtime, or before school. Add your meetings to your weekly time commitment. Be sure to stick to an agenda, and keep the meetings brief.

Divide the responsibilities. Some can be shared while others are handled individually.

- *The* **secretary** *organizes meetings and compiles all information found by the group.*

- *A* **community liaison** *researches local scholarship offerings and how to connect with business and community leaders as well as local politicians.*

Pro Tip

Club time is perfect for group brainstorming sessions. Remind each other of projects, experiences, and assignments to add to your Personal Search Engine Lists.

- *Your* **public relations** *team is responsible for outreach in and out of school, making sure to share information online, on bulletin boards, and with school leaders.*

Think outside of school. Meeting together at school is great for a scholarship club, but you could also organize a group at a community center or place of worship. You could even incorporate a mini scholarship club within another club or youth group.

Take it online. Create a Facebook group that members can post scholarships to. Start by inviting your friends... and see how the group expands beyond your community.

Share the wealth. When club members find scholarships that apply to younger students, make a point to forward the opportunity to your old middle school or elementary school. Reach out to the appropriate parent association and let them know that you have a great opportunity for that age group. Be sure to include the community service on your Personal Search Engine List.

No matter what form your group takes, or how you decide to include other students, you and your fellow members can only stand to benefit from the power of joining forces and working as a team.

FROM JEAN'S FILES

ONE SUMMER IN NEW YORK, I HELPED SET UP A SCHOLARSHIP CLUB AT THE ANTI-DEFAMATION LEAGUE. OVER A DOZEN STUDENTS PLEDGED TO HELP EACH OTHER FIND SCHOLARSHIPS. EACH WEEK BROUGHT DIFFERENT RESULTS, BUT EVERY STUDENT WAS MOTIVATED TO CONTRIBUTE. OVER THE COURSE OF FOUR WEEKS, MEMBERS COLLECTIVELY SHARED OVER 150 SCHOLARSHIPS.

A SPIRIT OF GIVING GOES A LONG WAY. WHEN YOU SHARE WITH OTHERS, OTHERS WANT TO SHARE WITH YOU! REMEMBER THAT YOU'LL ALWAYS FIND MORE WHEN YOU WORK TOGETHER.

Jean, I've had so much success this year, much of which is due to your superb tutelage. I've received two full-tuition scholarships and am being considered for two more. I have interned at the Model City Council Project where I spoke on an important social issue, and for Domenic Recchia's campaign for congress. I am a paid apprentice for the Museum of Jewish Heritage, and the director really liked my emphasis on how I would use my opportunities to help the world. I especially thank you for helping me articulate my "why me" statement. I come from a low income family, and money was always on my mind as I applied to colleges. I definitely don't want student loan debt. I guess I just want to let you know that your message is effective and impactful. My family and I thank you for all of your help.

—Amani M. 12th grade student

Chapter Fifteen

15 WAYS TO REDUCE COLLEGE COSTS

Your Money Mission is fully underway. You're going after every outside scholarship you can. The benefits of outside scholarships are numerous—reducing tuition bills, cutting college loan debt, and defraying supply and equipment costs. But you can DO MORE. Your biggest take away from this book is that *you own your choices*. Never accept college costs at face value. Ask questions. AIM FOR MORE.

There are many ways you can reduce the price tag of college. Use the cost-saving ideas that follow to stack the savings. Your tuition bill and your wonderful life-to-be will thank you.

#1 Financial Aid

The Free Application for Federal Student Aid (FAFSA) determines your eligibility for student financial aid. Nearly every student is eligible for some form of financial aid. The FAFSA should be completed *annually* by all current and prospective college students (undergraduate and graduate).

The FAFSA becomes available annually on October 1. Submit yours as early as possible. Do not put it off! Several opportunities, such as Pell Grants, are awarded on a first-come, first-served basis. The later you submit the FAFSA, the fewer opportunities are available to you.

After completing the FAFSA, you will receive a Student Aid Report (SAR), which provides potential eligibility for different types of financial aid, your Expected Family Contribution (EFC), and a summary of your application. Review the SAR for errors and make corrections as needed. In addition, the SAR is electronically sent to the colleges listed on your FAFSA, as well as to state agencies that award need-based aid.

The most common types of aid offered from the federal government as a result of completing a FAFSA are Pell Grants, Stafford Loans, Perkins Loans, and Work-Study.

TIP: You and your parents will need to provide information from recent income tax returns to file the FAFSA. Be sure to give your parents advance notice to gather their tax documents.

In addition, you will receive a financial aid letter from each school you listed on your FAFSA. Your letter will tell you if you are eligible for any grants. Public school grants are awarded by the state or federal government. Most private schools have established institutional grants (funded by the school). Either way, grants are awarded need-based and do not require repayment. You cannot qualify for grants without completing the FAFSA.

#2 College Specific Scholarships

Most colleges and universities offer merit, athletic, and special scholarships. Incoming students are often considered for scholarships upon admission. Some universities may offer a scholarship application. Once you have chosen a college, apply the principles of working smarter. Research your options and, if applicable, find out who won and why. Be sure you understand the eligibility criteria. If you desire a merit scholarship, focus on maintaining or boosting your GPA. In some cases, it may be beneficial to request a meeting, either in person, by phone, or by video conference. Either way, it never hurts to make a great impression and demonstrate your motivation.

#3 Start at a Community College

By attending a community college during your first one or two years of college, you can save thousands of dollars in tuition. You can apply that savings to a college or university for your last two years. Your future employer will only care about where you earned your degree. They aren't interested in where you started college.

Some students resist starting at a community college because they want the dorm, roommate, and on-campus existence for the full college experience. That's a fine choice to make. But if remaining free of student debt is important to you, a community college is a viable option toward succeeding in that goal.

> **TIP**: Make sure that the credits you earn from your classes at the two-year college will count at your four-year college so you can start out there as a junior. Find out if there are transfer agreements between where you are and where you want to go.

#4 Get a Job on Campus

Federal work-study provides part-time jobs to students with financial need. These jobs are limited to a set dollar amount that you may earn during that academic year (usually accomplished by working about 10 hours per week). However, there are many other employment opportunities on campus. Some are better than others. For example, a resident assistant (RA) is typically compensated with free or reduced housing as well as a stipend or meal plan. The College Board reports that the average cost of room and board in 2016-17 ranged from $10,440 at four-year public schools to $11,890 at private schools. Free or discounted room and board represents an enormous savings.

> **TIP**: Contact the student employment office at your college and ask about the highest paying student jobs. Find out how to apply and be sure to follow up with any leads.

#5 Become a Tutor or a Coach

TIP: Contact the local school district about your service or set up a profile on websites dedicated to offering tutoring or coaching services.

Take your academic, athletic, or creative superpowers and turn them into big bucks. Whether it's tutoring math, teaching piano, or providing coaching to a young football player, these positions traditionally earn more than on-campus jobs.

#6 Save Money on Textbooks

TIP: Ask early about reading lists required by your professors, and begin searching for the best prices as soon as possible.

College textbooks cost a fortune. But you're a smart shopper. When you comparison shop, you'll almost certainly find that the college bookstore is your worst option. Shop online, buy used, share with a friend, or buy an older edition (with the approval of your professor). Research the buy back options for books you don't intend to keep. Renting books is another option. No matter what you choose, stay away from the high prices on campus.

#7 Choose the Right Meal Plan

Most colleges offer several meal plans for you to choose from. Opt for the most basic. Then fill in any gaps with healthy snacks or quick meal items available at local grocery stores and big box discount stores. You can always upgrade to another plan if the most basic isn't working for you.

#8 Employee Discounts

TIP: Ask your parents to check job postings at local colleges and on websites dedicated to higher education jobs.

Institutions of higher education frequently offer reduced or free tuition to the children of employees. There are many different roles available on campuses: grounds and building maintenance, event planning, administrative, teaching, and many more. If you attend the school where your parent is employed, you could save a ton of money.

#9 Graduate ASAP

If your four-year program turns into a fifth year or sixth year, your costs will increase by thousands of dollars. Every semester you add costs more money. Conversely, if you take additional classes each semester or between semesters, you might shave off a semester or year and get that cap and gown ahead of time. To avoid adding semesters, consider the following tips:

- *Declare your major early so that you don't waste time taking unnecessary classes.*

- *Seek experiential learning opportunities or shadow someone in your potential field before college. These experiences will help inform your decision about potential majors and courses of study.*

- *If you change your major, early is better. If you do change later, be sure to understand your options, try not to lose credits, and take extra steps to graduate on time.*

- *Cut a semester or more off of your studies by enrolling in summer or winter terms.*

#10 Intern in Your Field

Internships often lead to full-time employment with the company after you graduate. Some companies even provide tuition reimbursement or student loan payoff assistance, making internships well worth looking into. Investigate companies in your chosen field that offer tuition reimbursement or student loan payoff assistance. Then, reach out to them to inquire about internship opportunities.

TIP: Connect with your academic adviser, the alumni office, and career services for leads on potential internships.

#11 Live Off Campus

Renting an off-campus apartment and preparing your own meals is almost always cheaper than living on campus. To make an informed decision, compare the cost of on-campus living to off-campus. Compare the price of room and board to your estimated costs for rent and groceries. If it's feasible for you to commute from home, that would represent even more savings.

My Choice is POWERFUL

#12 Don't Rule Out Private Schools

It is a fact that public colleges and universities have lower tuition and fees than private ones. Private institutions generally carry a higher sticker price, but those schools may use their endowment funds as they see fit. Lower income students in particular may be amply rewarded by exploring how much aid is offered by the private schools on their list.

#13 Earn College Credits Off Campus

If allowed by your school, take some courses at a less expensive college. Ask your adviser or the appropriate administrator at your institution about relationships your college has with other public colleges and which courses are eligible for transfer credits.

AIM FOR MORE

#14 Earn College Credits in Advance

Start cutting your college costs while in high school. If you earn an AP Exam score of 3 or higher, chances are you can receive credit, advanced placement, or both from your college. When you enter college with credit you've already earned through AP, you can save time and money. Additionally, look into summer programs,

TIP: Ask at your guidance office about college credit opportunities, which may be available as early as 10th grade.

community college courses, and online opportunities, and be certain to confirm whether the credits are transferable to your college.

#15 Combine Degrees

Some programs offer combined degrees. Students benefit from these programs because they offer a combination bachelor's/master's degree in a shorter amount of time. Instead of spending six or more years pursuing a bachelor's and master's, a student can get both in five years. Less time in college means more money saved.

TIPS: Talk to your college admissions department about established accelerated programs. If an accelerated program doesn't exist for your field of study, ask about having one customized for you.

WAIT! —THERE'S MORE!

Chapter Sixteen

INITIATING NEW SCHOLARSHIPS

Local scholarships, as you know, are great opportunities to pursue in your Money Mission. Let's assume you've rounded up a dozen scholarships offered by local businesses. You've also searched at your school and reached out to family members. You're feeling the glow of accomplishment, as you should. It's a great feeling, right? But there's more you can do. Always!

Never accept the status quo—you can always do more on your Money Mission. Expand your local reach and build your leadership skills at the same time by thinking outside the box.

Your Clubs

From drama to economics, you probably belong to any number of school clubs. A great group activity is to create a scholarship. Organize a fundraiser to fund the scholarship, and make the scholarship criteria unique to the club. For drama club, the scholarship winner could be chosen on best performance or best original play. An economics club might choose to require an essay that addresses a pressing global economic issue. The possibilities are endless, and it is a wonderful legacy to leave for your club.

Your Family

Ask family members to appeal to their employer to establish a new scholarship. You can help your relatives compose their request. Be sure to point out that when employers offer scholarships to children of employees, it builds loyalty.

Your Community

One incredible task your scholarship club (see Chapter 14) could take on is to encourage new scholarships in the community. It will take some work to network with community organizations and leaders, and you'll need to make a strong pitch, but as always, a few key strategies will help you get down to business.

TIME TO PUT THEM TO WORK!

Research local businesses that currently offer scholarships so that your club can readily show the myriad benefits of sponsoring a scholarship.

In your appeal, explain how businesses will directly benefit from sponsoring a scholarship.

For example, let them know that your club would alert local news outlets (newspaper, TV stations, school newspaper) and encourage them to cover businesses that sponsor scholarships awarded to local students. A $500 scholarship is a relatively inexpensive way to promote a business!

Pro Tip

For each scholarship pitch, explore how your skills were enhanced by the experience. Write about the experience on applications and essays.

- *Pledge to support the business as a group. Advocate their good deeds through social media, mention the business on your club website, have club t-shirts made that include businesses that sponsor scholarships in your community, tell your friends to support the business. There are so many ways to show your appreciation—make sure you do.*

This strategy benefits you and your fellow club members in so many ways. All of you will build confidence while improving your communication, public speaking, and presentation skills. And every bit of that is great practice for future interviews and presentations. You've probably already guessed it, but you'll need to add the experiences to your Personal Search Engine List.

As you work your Money Mission, remember to keep asking for more. You will learn valuable lessons that set you up for earning more—now and in the future. Keep going!

want more.

BE MORE.

find more.

DO MORE.

win more.

STACK The Dollars

Chapter Seventeen

MONEY MISSION: COLLEGE EDITION

The day you receive your high school diploma is a great day indeed. Celebrate! But don't forget about your Money Mission.

College-bound students playing the Waiting Game will stop looking for money after graduation. They believe the old myth that scholarships aren't available after high school. Good news for you: less competition.

If you are currently in college, there are many reasons to be motivated to search for scholarships.

Those reasons might include:

- You took out student loans to cover a portion of tuition.

I don't want The debt

- You plan to pursue an advanced degree or professional certification.

- You struggle to pay the many required additional expenses, such as supplies, travel, and incidentals.

- You are a nontraditional student.

- You just want more. That's all right too!

CONTINUING YOUR MONEY MISSION is so very, very important. Remember, you want your choices to be based on personal growth and opportunity, *not* financial burden.

The sad reality is that about half of all college students do not finish their degrees. Many of those students drop out because they cannot afford it. Or, as you've read earlier, many students take on burdensome college loans. That debt presents hefty post-graduation financial strains, which may mean deferring dreams such as vacations, advanced degrees, homeownership, and more.

Your meticulous files should already include scholarship opportunities just for college

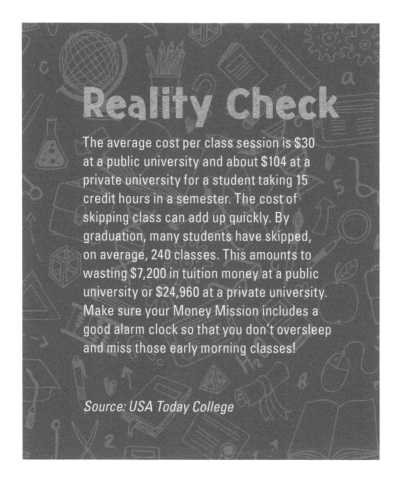

Reality Check

The average cost per class session is $30 at a public university and about $104 at a private university for a student taking 15 credit hours in a semester. The cost of skipping class can add up quickly. By graduation, many students have skipped, on average, 240 classes. This amounts to wasting $7,200 in tuition money at a public university or $24,960 at a private university. Make sure your Money Mission includes a good alarm clock so that you don't oversleep and miss those early morning classes!

Source: USA Today College

students. Make sure to continue to include application due dates on your schedule, alongside assignments, extracurricular activities, and work schedules. Make a Money Mission goal for college and stick to it. More applications will lead to more possibilities.

Your college Money Mission is going to look much like it did in high school but adapted to your new situation. Most scholarships for college students are geared toward majors and career paths.

The Student Loan Deal

It's not a deal. Public or private, student loan companies make money by putting you in debt, and often keeping you there. And so, student loans will always cost you money unless you get ahead of them. The only way to do that is to pay them off in full before they start earning interest.

Generally, your first loan payment will be due six months after you earn your degree. Depending on the type of loan, you can defer payments while you pursue advanced degrees (or based on need). But they don't go away. They will never go away until you satisfy them. As the years go by, interest adds up and loans cost you more and more.

Knock loans out as early and quickly as possible. Your savings will be enormous. As you continue to win scholarships in college, make a point to use the money to pay off loans early.

"I like that Jean's program helps me manage the application work within three 15-30 minute sessions per week."

—Kamirah G., 12th grade student

In Your Field: *Using a scholarship book index, locate and file scholarships granted to your particular field. Apply to them during each year of college.*

Online: *Conduct a targeted search on scholarship websites, using the "scholarships for college students" criteria.*

Connect With Alumni: *Ask your alumni office to connect you with alumni in your field. Contact these alumni by email or phone to ask what scholarships they received during college.*

I Will Do This!

Connect With Professional Associations: *Research the professional associations and organizations that are related to your field. Reach out to them to find out what scholarships opportunities are available to college students. While you're at it, ask about summer internship opportunities.*

You want to arrive at your future with the best financial situation. Continue to work a smart Money Mission during your undergraduate years and beyond.

Chapter Eighteen

REACH FOR THE STARS

"Right on! You really rocked this out! Keep going and stay with it!
Your money mission is now part of your life. Continue
adding to the pile, and GO GET MORE MONEY!"

—Jean

You have a full arsenal of strategies for cutting costs, being
a smart consumer, and finding money to pay for college. You
aren't playing the Waiting Game. You are on an ambitious
Money Mission that is motivated by the future that you desire.
Your college experience is going to be *life changing*—without
the burden of juggling jobs or taking on hefty loans to finance
it. The future never looked so bright!

25 Scholarship Strategies

CHAPTER 3

1 Create and maintain a Personal Search Engine List to guide you toward scholarship opportunities.

2 Compile your ready-to-go materials from past assignments to use for scholarship applications.

CHAPTER 4

3 Maximize your Big 6 categories for optimal opportunities.

CHAPTER 5

4 Apply to as many scholarships as possible.

5 Set a manageable weekly application goal.

CHAPTER 6

6 Apply to scholarships regardless of dollar amount.

7 Designate time in your weekly schedule to work on your Money Mission.

8 Create a plan of action for times when you have unexpected free time.

CHAPTER 7

9 Have family members inquire at their workplace, etc. about scholarship opportunities.

10 Research local scholarships that have the best chance of winning.

CHAPTER 8

11 Visit the college counselor office weekly to ask about new scholarship opportunities.

12 Learn what the local scholarship decision makers seek, and take action.

13 Connect with past scholarship winners and ask what they did to stand out.

CHAPTER 9

14 Use scholarship books to find scholarships that align with your Personal Search Engine List.

CHAPTER 10

15 Create and use an Application Timeline to stay on track with your Money Mission.

CHAPTER 11

16 Visit a variety of scholarship websites to search for opportunities.

17 Keep spam out your regular email inbox by creating a special email for scholarship searching.

CHAPTER 12

18 Ask your family and friends to let you know whenever they hear about a scholarship.

19 Give priority to time consuming applications. Fewer applicants means better odds.

CHAPTER 13

20 Craft a powerful "why me" statement to help you stand out from other applicants.

21 When appropriate, repurpose essays to economize your time.

CHAPTER 14

22 Start and participate in a scholarship club to maximize results and stay motivated.

CHAPTER 15

23 Stack savings on top of scholarship money by cutting college costs.

CHAPTER 16

24 Work with community businesses or organizations to create a new scholarship.

CHAPTER 17

25 Continue your Money Mission beyond high school graduation day.

That life? That dream? It's happening. It is *really* happening because you have made *choices* toward realizing your dreams!

It is impossible to predict how much scholarship money you will receive. As with everything else in life, there are no guarantees. But the thing is:

You cannot win a game that you are not playing.

You must be willing to accept uncertainty and commit to the process. Throughout this book you have discovered that you are your own best resource. Your unique characteristics and interests have pointed you toward the right opportunities. You've reflected on how you can do or be more. You've improved or maintained your GPA. And you've tried new extracurricular and leadership activities.

Through your Money Mission, you have become a stronger scholarship candidate, a stronger student, *a stronger person*. Your focus and drive will be a tremendous asset as you pursue your degree, and as you continue on your journey you will grow into a desirable job candidate.

You've locked on to the idea that *choice is the most powerful thing you own*. You've walked a path of self-discovery and self-improvement because you chose it. As your Money Mission takes you through college and beyond, your choices will continue to empower you.

"Jean's advice has been an eye-opener. When she started talking about students playing the Waiting Game, I immediately realized that was me. I now know that this process is up to me. If I want it, I need to work for it and make it happen."
—Yashara G., 12th grade student

If you opt to pass on these strategies, that is your prerogative. You can join the long line of other students who are playing the Waiting Game. In the end, getting money to pay for college is wildly unpredictable for those playing the Waiting Game. The risk is too big. If you don't actively seek money for college, you may be faced with staggering student loan debt or worse: dropping out of college. Betting on the Waiting Game might leave those beautiful dreams unfulfilled. Is that what you want?

Dealing With Rejection

As you apply for scholarships, rejection is bound to happen. Scholarship committees have hundreds of applications to consider. Win or lose, you will know that you put your best foot forward and presented yourself as an excellent candidate. Take this knowledge with you. When you can, try to turn your "no" applications into wins. Feel free to reapply as often as a scholarship allows. Never lose your momentum; turn every failure into a learning experience. Opportunity will reveal itself.

Stay Focused

When you imagine all that is coming your way, it's very natural to feel revved up and ready to go. Still, stick to your manageable weekly goal within your weekly schedule. Don't burn out by taking on too much at a time. Slow and steady wins the race! If you're bursting with enthusiasm, you could…

- Use your excitement to add to your Personal Search Engine List.

- Reflect on how much you've already accomplished in life!

- Find a quick scholarship or two to apply to immediately.

- Call up a few friends and get together for a Scholarship Club meeting.

As you work your Money Mission, be sure to take time to celebrate your wins! Let each choice, each action, and each win propel you to the next. Keep this book near for easy reference. Your future self will thank you.

Now, go reach for the stars! The choice is yours.

AFTERWORD

When I was a kid, my dad always said, "Much can be accomplished, if you are willing to work hard for it." Those words have stuck with me to this day. My parents taught my brother and me the value of hard work, and that working extra jobs is an opportunity and not a hardship. You could say that money missions were a core value in my upbringing.

I was the recipient of several generous scholarships in college, but my family and I still had to cover remaining costs with student loans. Knowing that those loans would need to be paid after graduation, I put myself in the best possible position for immediate employment upon graduating. This focus motivated me to complete six internships and work multiple part-time jobs in college.

During college a second pillar of my work ethic was established. I witnessed student after student expecting other people to open doors for them. This perplexed me, since it was, after all, the student's life. That's not to say that I didn't welcome and appreciate help along the way. However, I embraced the idea that, "If it is to be, it is up to me."

My professional life had an incredible jump start, and within a few years I was touring the United States as a presenter and motivator for large groups of students and parents. As it became clear that my audience was most concerned about the rising cost of college, I began to research scholarships. I quickly learned that there were more scholarship opportunities than I had ever dreamed of. I recognized that financial obstacles could be minimized if more students and parents knew more about outside scholarships. Rather than paying for college costs, college funds could be redirected to buy a home, start a business, or any number of other possibilities.

Although there are no guarantees of winning scholarships, a personal commitment to applying for as many as possible will improve student outcomes. When I joined Connections101 in 2008, I was able to present my Scholarship Strategies message to thousands of high school students. It has been my privilege to assist countless students in finding their way to a Money Mission. More recently, I was presented with an opportunity to cast a wider net—and reach students beyond NYC—by putting my message in print. The book in your hands is the outcome of those efforts, and I sincerely hope that the information I've presented will help guide your choices as you work toward your dreams!

Jean O'Toole

Elementary and Middle School Student Scholarships

Angela Award
Open to any female resident of the United States, Canada, or U.S. Territories in grades 5-8. Must be involved in or have a strong connection to science.

www.nsta.org/about/awards.aspx?lid=tnav#angela

Gloria Baron Prize
Open to young leaders (ages 8-18) who have made a significant positive difference to people and the environment.

www.barronprize.org/

Jack Kent Cooke Foundation Young Scholars Program
Open to high academic performing 7th grade students with financial need.

www.jkcf.org/ysp

We the Future Contest
Open to students (K-5) who submit a poem or holiday card.

www.constitutingamerica.org

Recommended Resources for College Planning & Scholarship Searching

College Board
www.collegeboard.org

FinAid
www.finaid.org

Road2College
www.road2college.com

BrokeScholar
www.brokescholar.com

SallieMae
www.salliemae.com/college-planning

Peterson's
www.petersons.com

US News & World Report
www.usnews.com/education

Naviance
www.naviance.com

College Connection
www.collegescholarships.com

CollegeView
www.collegeview.com

U.S. Department of Education
www.ed.gov

The Ultimate
Scholarship Book
Kelly Tanabe

Scholly
(mobile app)

Wacky Scholarships

Over the years, we have found some seriously wacky scholarship opportunities. The following is a sampling of our favorites. Scholarships are ever-changing, so some of these won't be around forever, but maybe these ideas will inspire a wacky opportunity for your unique traits. For an updated list, please visit www.connections101.com.

Bonnie 3rd Grade Cabbage Program
Open to 3rd grade students.

REQUIREMENT: Grow a cabbage plant.

www.bonniecabbageprogram.com

Car Covers Scholarship
Open to undergraduate and graduate students.

REQUIREMENT: Write an essay on "How to make your car last forever."

www.carcovers.com/resources/scholarship/

Do-Over Scholarship
Open to students 13 or older.

REQUIREMENT: Write about what "do-over" you'd like to have in your life.

www.unigo.com/scholarships/our-scholarships/do-over-scholarship

ES-Zone Healthy Living Scholarship
Open to high school and college students.

REQUIREMENT: Write an essay about the importance of eating healthy foods.

www.electricsmokerzone.com/scholarship

E-Waste Scholarship
Open to students in 9th grade through graduate school.

REQUIREMENT: Write a 140 character statement about e-waste.

www.digitalresponsibility.org/ewaste-scholarship

Make It With Wool Contest
Open to all ages.

REQUIREMENT: Construct and model garment(s).

www.nationalmakeitwithwool.com

Parry & Pfau Left-Handed Scholarship
Open to high school, undergraduate or graduate students.

REQUIREMENT: Video submission answering, "Why is it better to be left-handed than right-handed?"

www.p2lawyers.com/scholarship

Pelican Water Sustainability Scholarship
Open to undergraduate and graduate students.

REQUIREMENT: Instagram post related to water conservation.

www.pelicanwater.com/scholarship.php

Project Yellow Light Scholarship
Open to high school juniors and seniors and undergraduate students.

REQUIREMENT: Create a PSA to discourage distracted driving.

www.projectyellowlight.com

Stuck at Prom Scholarship Contest
Open to students 14 years or older.

REQUIREMENT: Create and wear complete prom attire and accessories with Duck brand duct tape.

www.stuckatprom.com

Tall Clubs International Scholarship
Open to first-year-college-bound students under 21 with a minimum height of 5'10" (women) or 6'2" (men).

REQUIREMENT: Nomination by your local TCI chapter.

www.tall.org/tci-foundation.html

Vegetarian Resource Group Scholarship
Open to graduating high school students.

REQUIREMENT: Promote vegetarianism at school and write an essay.

www.vrg.org/student/scholar/htm

Zombie Apocalypse Scholarship
Open to students 13 or older.

REQUIREMENT: Describe your action plan if your school became overrun with zombies.

www.unigo.com/scholarships/our-scholarships/zombie-apocalypse-scholarship

INDEX

ACKNOWLEDGMENTS

This book would not have been possible without the support of Ken Metz and Forrest King. I am deeply grateful not only for their belief in this project, but also for their belief in me. Without them I would not have had the honor to impact so many thousands of lives during my tenure with Connections101. Through this book, they have helped me extend my voice to reach beyond the school auditoriums, libraries, classrooms, and gymnasiums. Ken's tireless energy and devotion to opening life possibilities for all who work with him is an unending source of inspiration to live a life of service to others.

Misty Boundless Wilt and Alicia Zadrozny helped me bring this project to fruition. Their guidance along the way was invaluable and their creativity aided in giving voice to my vision for this book.

Countless teachers, guidance counselors, and administrators have welcomed me into their schools over the past decade to share my scholarship information with their students. Every minute of the school day is valuable, and I am humbled that they chose to designate time for my workshops and assemblies. Special thanks to Linda King, Nancy Trapido, Peg Kiely, Sandra Burgos, Brandon Simmons, Maria Spagnuolo, Danielle Tourdo, Barbara Correnti, and Camille Geathers for their commitment to their students and to bringing my message and resources to their schools.

Thank you to all of the students who made the choice to take action and start scholarship money missions. They inspire me daily to continue sharing my message despite endless hours in the car, fighting traffic and traveling through rough weather. They keep me going and their success stories inspire other students with hope that success can be possible for them too.

I have been gifted by remarkable mentors along my journey. I would not be celebrating the success of my many years of research and work without the influence of my fellow youth motivational speakers and trainers from Making It Count. Their guidance is with me as I take the microphone in front of every audience. They encouraged me to discover my voice and use it to impact others. They saw potential within me when I didn't see it myself. I especially thank Terri Wilson for pushing all of us to use our voices to help young people change their worlds.

Ken Mossman, Jason Sirois, Ginger Merritt, Carey Urban, Karen Giorgis, Lisa Lansing, and Krystal Lafountain have been my cheerleaders from the beginning. Their support of "all things Jean" moves me to tears of joy. I recognize that the completion of this project was yet another mountain that they each helped me climb.

I am grateful most of all to my incredible family who imprinted my core belief that hard work and commitment can yield tremendous reward in life. I thank my parents, Lillian and Michael Fedora, for encouraging me to create my own individual road map for my life, and my brother, Mike Fedora, for reminding me that celebration and joy should be savored after all the striving. Most importantly, I thank my incredible partner and loving husband Stephen, who inspires me daily with his own impact on students as a high school teacher. His presence in my life is a gift from God, and a reminder that every day is an opportunity to positively impact the future of the world by leaving a lasting impression on a student.

ABOUT THE AUTHOR

 Jean O'Toole grew up in Western Massachusetts in a family focused on money missions. She received a bachelor's degree in Arts Administration from Wagner College in 1997. Early in her professional life she toured the United States as a presenter and motivator for large groups of students and parents. As it became clear that her audience was most concerned about the rising cost of college, in 2003 Jean began researching what would become *Scholarship Strategies*. In 2005 she was accepted into the prestigious Monster's Making It Count student speaker program, which helped her fine-tune her message for larger audiences of students and parents. In 2008 she joined Connections101 in New York City. Connections101 is a youth empowerment company specializing in motivational tools for outside scholarship searching. Through their support, her scholarship strategy program has become a staple for many high schools. Jean currently resides in New Jersey with her loving husband Stephen, their two dogs Thelonious and Dude, and Nina the cat.

www.connections101.com

CPSIA information can be obtained
at www.ICGtesting.com
Printed in the USA
JSHW011657080121
10765JS00005B/73